I0148678

THE CHRONICLES

THE CHRONICLES

❈

poems

RAMÓN GARCÍA

RED HEN PRESS | *Pasadena, CA*

The Chronicles
Copyright © 2015 by Ramón García
All Rights Reserved

No part of this book may be used or reproduced in any manner whatsoever without the prior written permission of both the publisher and the copyright owner.

Book layout by Jessica Weber
Author photo by David Garza

Library of Congress Cataloging-in-Publication Data
García, Ramón, 1967–
  [Poems. Selections]
  The chronicles / Ramón García.—First edition.
    pages ; cm
  ISBN 978-1-59709-428-3 (softcover : acid-free paper)
  I. Title.
  PS3607.A724A6 2015
  811'.6—dc23
                    2014037134

Ahmanson Foundation, the Dwight Stuart Youth Fund, the Los Angeles Department of Cultural Affairs, Sony Pictures Entertainment, The Los Angeles County Arts Commission, the National Endowment for the Arts, the Pasadena Arts & Culture Commission and the City of Pasadena Cultural Affairs Division partially support Red Hen Press.

First Edition
Published by Red Hen Press
www.redhen.org

ACKNOWLEDGMENTS

Grateful acknowledgment is made to the MacDowell Colony, the Virginia Center for the Creative Arts, and The Ragdale Foundation, where some of the poems in this collection were written or revised, and to the editors of the following publications in which these poems appeared:

Ambit 181 (UK), "Looking for God in Los Angeles"; *Borderlands: Texas Poetry Review*, "The Water Speaks of Narcissus"; *Crab Orchard Review*, "Passion Play"; *Eclipse: A Literary Journal*, "Larry Levis, Valley Poet"; *In The Grove*, "The Southern Pacific Railroad Train"; *The Los Angeles Review*, "Cassandra: South Central Gangsta Girl Prophecy"; *Mandorla: New Writing from the Americas*, "Jesus Predicts his Death," "Lion's Bridge"; *Margie: The American Journal of Poetry*, "Sleeping Beauty"; *Poetry Salzburg Review* (Austria), "Sycorax"; and *Quarry West 25*, "Mental Health Worker at Crestwood Manor" and "Modesto."

I am grateful for the support of Saskia Hamilton, Alexa Altman, Chon Noriega, Harry Gamboa Jr., Ricky Rodriguez, Suyapa Portillo, Patssi Valdez, Espie Valverde, John Valadez, Rita Gonzalez, Ondine Chavoya, Sandra De La Losa and Yreina Cervantez Francisco X. Alarcon, Jeffery Renard Allen, Molly Bendall, Elena Karina Byrne, Pablo Capra, Lorna Dee Cervantes, Susana Chávez-Silverman, Eric-Christopher Garcia, David Garza, Elizabeth Horan, Louis Jacinto, Richard McDowell, Joe Medina, Marisela Norte, Camille Norton, Alicia Partnoy, Kene Rosa, Terese Svoboda, Helena Maria Viramontes, Terry Wolverton, Peter Woods, Gail Wronsky, Cecilia Woloch, David William Foster and Maythee Rojas. Many thanks to the squirrels—María Elena Gaitán, Gronk, and Tanner Goldbeck. I wish to thank the members of the Glass Table Collective for the work we do together. With much appreciation and heartfelt gratitude I want to thank Jerry Rodriguez, Benjamin Figueroa, José Guttierrez, Caroline Le Duc, David Leclerc, Sirena Pellarolo, Ricky Ridecos, Breny Mendoza, Anna Sandoval, Mary Pardo and Zeeva Natasha Zazhinne—thank you for being who you are. I also wish to thank my extended family in Modesto.

For David Leclerc

Indescifrablemente forman parte
del tiempo, de la tierra y del olvido.

Indecipherably they form a part
of time, of earth and of oblivion.

— *Jorge Luis Borges*

CONTENTS

I. SACRED TEXTS

II. GENEALOGIES

III. THE CHRONICLES

THE CHRONICLES

I. SACRED TEXTS

FAIRY-TALE CHRONICLES

The Frog Prince Triptych

i. The Frog to the Princess

Not for me the enchanted kingdom
of the human.
I prefer the gutters
where my obscure green origins thrive
pulsing with the earth
until death, that other perfection,
joins me to the rudimentary mire
wherein I am at home.

Your beauty has been bred
in sleep, virginity and curses.
Your lips are impersonal, authoritative,
they glisten with exile.

I won't be mirror to your luxuries,
kin to prettiness.
Proudly I wear my mucky nakedness,
slippery as lust—
the inheritance of roots, leaves, darkness
and water.
Hear my croaking, the brotherhood it becomes—
that's who I am, a frog among frogs,
tenors of unruly orgies in the puddles.

The refusal of my kiss will
madden you.

The mirrors and the corpses of your realm
will replicate your lovely face.
But I'll be underground, undoing
your possessions, in the country
you have trampled on
whose singing
you never could suppress.

ii. The Princess to the Frog

You traded your pond
for my pillow.
And since then
memory and yearning
have marred the marriage bed.
The refinements of the prince
are wanting—
unlike the taste of common earth
and mudslides
on your skin.

You awakened remote seasons,
violent rains, the hidden marshes
beyond my ordered gardens.
The mud and messiness
are worth more
than my father's gold.

Now, in your princely state,
you give me patience,
bottomless sophisticated silence.
But I long for the spell
that made you a son of storms
and cyclical backwash
rousing me to precious fears
and rare hungers.

Night comes with
the crooning of the frogs—
a torment.
How the opulence of my kingdom
is wrecked by those choruses amplifying
my loneliness!
Now that I have heard the beauty of your song,
now that it has gone back to the frogs.
And you are no longer one of them.

iii. The Prince Remembers Being a Frog

I remember the spell
as a passage, a sort of dream, unearthing:
a well, a golden ball, water, mud and
nights of singing. Revelry and discovery
among comrades I came to love.
And the princess asking me favors.
And the princess making promises
she never meant to keep.

To be back where I belong—
but it's not the same anymore.
The princess sulks and resents me,
a curse confirming
my place as a man.

When the frogs sing
my flesh stirs with the homesick wounds
of their clandestine pleasures.
And I long to be with them
and of them,
frantic, rowdy, multiple,
without a kingdom
without this man's body.

Snow White

The magic mirror courts the evil stepmother's madness.
It never breaks or reveals her face at seventy.

Snow White is beyond the mountains.
She's survived the stepmother's murderous plot,
Serviceable as a nun in a cottage filled to capacity
With the dwarfs' stunted testosterone.
But her beauty still wins out.

The witch-mother is again at her mirror
Slapping the same damn question at it.
Doesn't the mirror get tired of her,
Of telling the truth?
Even God would relent after a while,
Throw a white lie at her to shut her up,
But not her mirror
It blurts out the truth no matter what.

She's not giving up, vain mother of iniquity.
She must be number one in the empire of mirrors,
The dominion of her dictatorship.
Now she's a mad scientist in the laboratory of narcissism
Transforming Eve's apple into the final solution.
And Snow White, that poor pretty thing,
She's stubborn and dumb and won't listen
To her midget protectors.
She eats half of the apple,
The poisoned half, the half that kills.

She dies, of course,
And is laid to rest in a glass coffin,
Is put on display for her admirers.
She doesn't decompose, not her,
Like Evita Perón, she rewrites truth
In the glamorous lexicon of death.

A prince, her alarm clock,
Arrives to give her the big wake-me-up,
To kill the stepmother in a marriage of blood
To seal man and fairy-tale wife.

Snow White inherited the magic mirror.
But she and the prince, like Theosophist spouses,
Were compelled to interrogate it,
As Snow White's stepmother had.
"Mirror, Mirror, on the wall, who in this realm is the fairest of all?"
"You, my prince, are as pretty as the princess,
Your hair golden and your white smile perfect,
But beyond the mountains and the sea
Is a black man more handsome
And bigger where it counts."
Snow White fell to dreaming of Nubian love
And gorgeous mulatto babies.
The dwarfs, her old consorts, tried to stop her,
But she took the next boat out of town.

It was a Jim Crow country she went to
And she soon learned about taboos and hate.
She couldn't marry her black man,
Who loved her but had to get away from her.

She married a doctor of her race
And many years later
She looked into an ordinary suburban mirror
And remembered she had once
Been a beautiful vulnerable girl
In a country of more personal evils.

Sleeping Beauty

Of what were Sleeping Beauty's dreams made?
The fleshless dreams of a virgin?
She came from a blond, cold country, a cursed
puritanical region.

She was beautiful,
crystalline and pure
as an uncontaminated snowflake,
inviolate.

There was a witch, an evil prophesy,
because beauty has its enemies.

There was an accident, her blood was shed,
just barely, a drop as big as a teardrop,
enough to seal the landscape of her fate.

She slept uninterrupted as the dead,
the years like an unbroken night.

There was a kiss, flesh awakening flesh,
a warm trembling breaking the blank spell of sleep.

The depths of her shuddered
and she came to, she awakened.

But she didn't know who she was.

Bluebeard's Castle

A blue beard, imagine!
What was considered repulsive
most attracted me—his gaudy distance
from run-of-the-mill men.

I didn't take into account
his castle, his opulence,
what my conniving sisters craved
for overlooking his freakishness,
his beauty.

And yet he chose them,
because I loved his apartness,
the luxurious loneliness
of his deformities.

Nothing would have led me
to that most protected, isolated
of rooms. I know the place too well.
It's there I had come from
and tried to escape,

where I am condemned
to stay, helplessly faithful
to the most violated victim,
his heart.

Rumpelstiltskin

The question is
who is that little man
and where did he come from?
How did he acquire his Midas touch?
Was it a gift of nature or the gods?

He is a breeder of gold.
Why does he want a baby so badly?
Most men can live on gold alone,
        why not him?

The question is: does he look
and sound like Truman Capote?
If he were taller, would he still
hunger so much for fatherhood?

Where magic and power conspire
a man's name must remain secret
from the fair sex, whom we all know
suffer from a Christopher Columbus complex.

His gold-spinning powers had made
her a queen. But like any married couple,
or tourists bartering in a foreign country
they had to make a deal,
come to an agreement.
Like a little girl who wants a doll
the little man wanted a baby.

But she tried to fool him, and in the end
discovered his real name,
the last uncolonized beach of his soul.
Although it was a foreign language to her
a sort of gobbledygook, his name was his history
and his land.
And he vowed to recover it.

The Bird in the Robber Bridegroom

I was kept in a cage
in a house of murder and rape.

My kindness had no bounds.
I convinced the virgin maiden
it had only been a dream when I warned
her out of death's house.

The robber bridegroom's in jail,
and the maiden-bride is safe,
but I was left in the cage
in the terrible company of
all the violence I witnessed.

I was a dream to the bride-to-be
but the men I sent to jail
        still imprison me.

THE JESUS CHRONICLES

John the Baptist

Oh, how the waters call me!
Oh, how God's turbulent depths
Say to my body:
"This is you and your savior."

My hands caress his gift, the water.
I bathe the flesh in mysteries, in ritual,
A flooding of holiness—baptism—
My appointed job
In the wildernesses of Christ.

I am the man of waters,
Of secret currents and tears.
I know submersion in immortality,
The divine drowning in Jesus.

Thirsty animals come to lap the water
Where I do my holy work.
Birds trill as I bathe with repentant
Sinners in the rivers.
Sometimes their song enters the light, the clouds
Darken—and I think I feel another kind of duty
Breaking through, a love that could
Exist beyond the water's shadowings.

Then the silence returns,
The light sunders itself
From the chorus of birds in the trees,
And I know the Holy Spirit is present
In the blazing stillness of the water.
Then I get back to patiently doing my job.

Jesus Walks on Water

It is true that Jesus walked upon the sea.
Like an elementary school kid at traffic patrol,
he signaled the waters to STOP
and the sea flattened out
like the San Joaquin Valley suburbs.
Jesus slid over the water
like an ice-skating champ.
It was beautiful, a ten
according to the judges,
the disciples who made him a winner.

It is true that Jesus walked upon the sea.
The waters have never forgotten.
It was a singular moment of peace,
pure life stilling into life.
Then the sea resumed its ancient anarchy,
its trinity of violence, obscurity,
and faithless infinity.
Jesus finished his magic tricks and the old
troubles returned—
the waves at war
nonstop,
a manic motor
running on the dreams of murderers.

Yes, it is true that Jesus walked on water.
Look upon the surf and you will see
the absence of Jesus,

hope devouring itself
in the waves' surging waste—
memory and time—
what Jesus left behind,
the day he came
to hand out his miracle wares.

Lazarus

From the cave of death,
        the breathless dark,
he brought me back.
        Because he was a god

he owned my flesh,
        and my entire afterlife.
And wanted more—
        faith and followers,

the puppet proof of his
        powers. On the stage
of resurrection, deprived of a script,
        I was his star. I bore

        a remote pallor:
all the secret heavens
        he imprisoned,
the loving god.

Jesus and the Whore

Jesus was at a banquet and a local
whore came to see him.
She poured fragrant oils and sex-tired tears
on his feet, and lowered her lips
to touch his hairy toes.

She kissed his feet like little girls
kiss teddy bears, with innocence and devotion.
On her knees, she looked up at him
and saw he was not wearing any underwear
underneath his white robe, that minimalist wedding dress.
His crotch was a Platonic country
where she could be a good citizen.

Jesus, that sin banker, meant business—
"Your sins are forgiven. I will marry
your past to my needs and you shall be saved.
Be free, my little bird! The cage of lust
is not your home, bliss
is no longer prisoner of your body.
Go, my little sperm machine,
I have made you as pure as a five-year-old girl."

The ex-whore went away to remember Jesus.
Jesus went to die, to do what he had to do.
They remained forever faithful,
convert and spouse freed of their pleasures.

Jesus Predicts His Death

I see the comatose blue
Of the sea, a backdrop
For the parade of my marvels.
I see deserts' oases become
Menacing as I approach them.
I feel forty days and forty nights
Burning their forty suns and forty
Moons inside me.
I sense my absence on earth
Replaced by bread and wine.
I feel the betraying
Kiss that is love
Despite all crime.
I feel the weight of
The cross that will be
My immortal home.
I hear pigs, a demon choir
Singing the swan song of lust.
I feel motherly and sisterly
Tears on my flesh and their
Love salts sting.
I feel saliva on
Flesh and I cannot tell
If it is the taste of a lover
Or the spit of an enemy.
I hear a terrible hammering,
The nailing of violence
Upon flesh and memory.

I see thorns and a lush
Flowering that could be
Roses or blood.
I see my father's heaven darken
The shadow of my ascent
In Golgotha
And I hear myself
Asking one question
That will be answered
By the silence of the sky.

Judas

Who knows why he did it?
Why he sold Jesus away like an old
        chair at a yard sale?

Perhaps he was in debt,
    à la Madame Bovary, hysterical
and desperate. He had been living beyond
    his means, an incurable romantic.

Maybe he was just greedy.
Is that why he seems so real,
        so enigmatic yet familiar?

Could it be that he couldn't resist
a kiss flavored with rare
        exquisite betrayal?

Maybe Judas was suicidal from the beginning,
    that's always a possibility,
        that he was a sad cynic
    had given up on people
        and people's gods.

Ambitious and mediocre, he wanted
        fame and immortality
            at any price.
He couldn't sell forgiveness, or love.

Pietà

All lovers are complicit
in gestures of
dying son and loving mother.

Whoever has longed
has lived this scene:
the dying pose
the look of grief.

Whoever has lusted
has known the son's wounded limbs
the mother's inexhaustible claim.

Whoever has loved
has assumed a surrender
a sublime arrangement:

the bearing of beautiful loss.

MYTHIC CHRONICLES

In the Labyrinth

I walked the walled-in trails
tracing the dead in every step
the Others who had taken
the same fatal

Detours.
Brothers and sisters
had faced the tyrant.

Victims or martyrs?
They had kept
their clothes on.

But I, coming upon
his brutality, offered
bare limbs, an unprotected heart.

And tasting the tenderness
of flesh, unleashing longing
he lost his hunger

And pointed the way out.

The Water Speaks of Narcissus

I, who was complete,

Was visited by the youth's face
    The beauty

    That made me mirror
    Instrument
I, who had been transparent

Where his submerged eyes were lost in adoration
Fish circle implacably and jump to choke on air
Forgetting I am home to them

Where once
    He installed his image
The depths are frigid
    Algae expire

    The flowers
    That bloomed
Because I gave myself to them
Make me their poison

Except the flower that is said to be
    The boy: it blooms
At the edges of my reaching,
    Transfixed by yearning
And refuses to release me.

Medusa's Men

My sovereign face
destined to be offered to men, who
because unbrave and strangers
to mystery, populate this deadscape:

island museum of arrested bodies
alien to my keen lust
the searing revelations of my trust.
They, being men, would have chosen

a moderate longing, mother-full eyes,
a sisterly mouth, feminine familiarity
promising children.
Not this wild

messiness snaking my head,
or my introverted stare, open to
deformity, estrangement, ecstasy.
Sterile and stranded,

memory cannot move them
or dead blood root them back
to the flesh. They have perfected
their fears, and all these years

burden my estate with what
they have escaped—women and themselves.

Orpheus, Dead in Los Angeles

A waterless graffitied canal
the city's version of a river
will carry Orpheus's head

singing in lyrical Spanish
songs of struggle
and rejected seductions:

(the neutered plastic flowers
made in China,
and the eunuch grasses
didn't respond to his advances,

and he was already confused!)

Poor Orpheus
pursued
under attack

and now dismembered

who will gather
his melodies?
the lyre's disjointed praises?

dear poets, dear brothers
you sing of exile
while the Mexican roses open their

promiscuous petals
and the palm fronds obey
your every sound

he is gone
down that river
of concrete, of emptiness
underneath the freeway overpasses

there is no shrine at the end
of his beheaded journey

yet, hear me
who live in phantom metropolises
but are citizens of his flesh

let his oblivion continue us

there was as much love
in his songs
as in his silence

Cassandra: South Central Gangsta Girl Prophecy

That's right
Name's La Cassy, Cassandra,
Y Que!

And since you asked
I'll tell you what's coming down.

You think you've seen riots?
You ain't seen shit.
Little *broncas*, little shoot-outs,
Forget it.

We're in for some real fire.
Bullets are going to make music
Ghetto birds are going to drop from the sky
Their searchlights hit ground
And for the first time
The sky will be the sky
Without the helicopters hunting us down
Getting in the way of the stars.

You think I'm talking crazy
But look around—
This ain't no paradise
Even the palm trees are beat up like old whores.

There'll be screaming and wailing
Smoke stinking up the city with fear

Police sirens ripping through
Pent-up darkness, the city's betraying peace.

I'll die here like I lived here
By the gun and in flames
I always knew
I'd be taking this city down with me
That it couldn't be otherwise.

Sycorax

I mother deformity
The imperfect language
Of perfected curses

Darkest abandonment
You populate
Islands and continents

Oh, fathers of plunder
I give you Caliban

He is broken, various
Shards of a mirror
Made to reflect
Your slashed eyes
Your misaligned monstrous

Mouths:

Inescapable offspring
Of crime

Marilyn

In Castroville, California, there is a gay bar
Called Norma Jean's, where a girl
Who would become a Goddess
Was waiting tables when she won
The first annual Miss Artichoke beauty contest.

This is a myth, but could have some validity.
Marilyn Monroe came from those artichoke fields
You see when you step out of the bar and leave
The vaqueros dancing on the colored dance floor,
The Mexican drag queens—a Paquita la del Barrio, a Thalía—
Sitting on barstools downing tequila shots
And the pretty boys snorting meth in the bathroom stalls.

You can leave the wax museums and gay bars
The libraries and DVD stores, all the places
Where her dreams have infiltrated

But you cannot escape her
Seduction.

She is the Whitman of a world
That has abandoned him.
The song of gay teenagers
Presidents, scholars, hustlers,
Writers and auto mechanics.

Poor Marilyn, she loved too much!
From continent to continent—

A song for the closed roads of the spirit.

II. GENEALOGIES

The Two Childhoods

I.

I remember a boy mesmerized by white butterflies,
Giant white petals riding the winds
Kite-like,
Through the still bright hours of interchangeable afternoons
In the town he was to leave.

Other things I remember:
The plaza at night, cobblestone streets,
Christ's naked bleeding
Inside the cold 19th century cathedral,
The wimples of the nuns at school,
Rivers, forests, fields,
Afternoon funerals of men killed
In the dimness of the surrounding mountains,
The penis of an older boy neighbor masturbating in the haystacks,
Scorpions, lizards . . .

Orville Wright elementary school,
The block letters of the alphabet
Lined atop the classroom's chalkboard,
The tedious nights of the suburbs,

Longing for the animated
Darkness of Coalcomán
Peopled with devils, ghosts, legends,
The disemboweled sky.

II.

There will be a self-evident death,
Ending, quite matter-of-factly,
What I have made of the Modesto suburbs
And the cities lived in and traveled through.

And there is the other death,
That would have been mine
If I had not left
A Mexico grown foreign to this
Other life that became who I am.

The Statues

They are still there,
Inside the church in Coalcomán,
At Saint Stanislaus in Modesto

The apostle Peter and John the Baptist.

Christ bleeds
Postured in beckoning
Suffering nakedness.

Look at Mary, virgin mother of God
And poor Mary Magdalene in the afterlife of sin
Made equals by beauty's injustice
The artistry of human likeness.

How they impersonate immortality!
The soulless stand-ins—
Duplicates of a heavenly race
Blessed conspiracy of identity theft.

Baroque, their patience;
They wait in the catechisms of memory
In childhood cathedrals of forgotten music.

Thousands of sermons
Have not penetrated their deafness.
Year after year, roses and calla lilies
Garden under their delicate feet,

Votive candles and prayers flicker,
Frankincense blooms mild smoke,
The prayers fade, but their indifference
Remains, petrified deep in the absence of flesh,
Fixing them to agelessness.

Afflicted women longingly
Look up to their fine consoling faces.

And the nervous boy,
Staring at Saint Paul's
Pure lacquered skin,
Christ's bleeding limbs
In the fog of scented air—

Into the bedroom of nights
He will take them
In the unholy cities of manhood
He'll know them
Defaced, shattered, ruined.

MODESTO

The Baptist church buildings
occupy half a block downtown.
Suited-up Mormons and zoot-suited-up homeboys
ride religiously—
the holy bikes and lowrider Chevys
cruise for conversion
in good and bad neighborhoods.

The missionary jingle of the ice cream truck
has its regular following
of afternoon children.
Morning Mormons knock on anonymous doors.
Supermarkets, fast food restaurants and mini-malls
sprout continuously, throughout the town,
a video store and a church
in every neighborhood.

On the corner of 1st and Main
near the Southern Pacific Railroad tracks
the taco van is open all night.
Down the street is the Estrella Azul bar
wailing rancheras until morning.
Further down is the X-rated bookshop
and the Salvation Army store.
The KKK has its headquarters on the outskirts of town.

The neon signage of cheap motels
beckons the fast lanes of the highway.

Semi-trucks hoot grinding whistles
twenty-four hours a day.
The smoke spewed by the canneries
ascends under the blank skies.

PASSION PLAY

Christ is a teenage Mexican boy in
a wig, thin, unshaven, in a faux
crown of thorns. Surrounding him,
the women of Judea are girls from
the church's youth group; they
wear Technicolor Biblical dresses
and turban-like shawls à la
Hollywood Mary Magdalene.
Pontius Pilate, in a white bed sheet
toga and Gap sandals, orders
Jesus's death. The parking lot of
St. Jude church becomes the streets
of Jerusalem, the *Via Dolorosa*
where Roman soldiers—puberty
stricken boys in skirts—flog Jesus
with black leather whips. The Son
of God, fake blood running from
fake wounds, falls in anguish once
again as he's lead to Golgotha, a
mound of dirt beyond the parking
lot. The girls follow, simulating
grief, they kneel to recite New
Testament passages, hiding girlish
giggles behind their colorful
shawls of sorrow. Then the
soldiers rope Christ's wrists to his
wooden cross, and hoist him up
under the skies of the suburbs.

"Lord, why hast thou forsaken
me?" the boy mutters. Mary,
Martha and Magdalene lift woeful
eyes at the martyred brown boy in
a loosened loincloth revealing the
toned limbs of a soccer player:
Oh, symbol of salvation! The
girls' theatrics stop and pose into
tableau—the audience claps.

FIELD WORK

We rode in the back of a truck, my brother and I,
With the Mexican men who worked the fields.
Packed into the shell of a truck bed,
In the searing afternoon of a Modesto summer,
The men didn't speak.

It was Mom's idea
That if my brother wanted a car
He should know what working for it meant,
That we should see for ourselves what it would be like
If we didn't study, as Dad said,
To escape the hard work that we would otherwise inherit.

Days in the hot fields picking peaches
Were to teach us a lesson.
Abuelito agreed, and came with us.
He crouched down on the truck bed with the men,
As he had done for many years
As a *bracero* in the Sacramento fields.
Those times had never left him,
And he wanted us to know them
So that we, in our silly youth,
Designer jeans and hair gel,
Would face the seriousness of money.

My brother climbed the ladder with a
Tin bucket to his chest, strapped to his back,
In a hurry, he picked the peaches, filled his bucket,

And ran to fill the Jacuzzi-sized wooden crate.
He did OK, for a kid who wasn't used to it.
And I did badly. Unsteady on the ladder,
And slow, I fell behind my brother
And the men who knew the tricks, the work
And how to tolerate the boredom,
The sun's hate, the redolent disgust of peach fuzz,
The late afternoon's slow simmering madness.

I didn't go back another day, but my brother did,
For two whole weeks, until he earned the half
Of the twelve-hundred dollars Mom and Dad
Wouldn't give him for a used Toyota.
My failure in the fields was joked about.
And *abuelito*, though he tried not to show it,
Pitied me.

And those men, owned by the sweet sweltering
Fruit of scorching afternoons and what their body
Could buy for them of survival,
I don't remember them, except for one,
Thin, dark, and too sad for his young age,
Like *abuelito* once,
I see them—the young man, my grandfather,
When I drive by the fields even now,
The lesson continuing, but unlearning itself.

Sentimental Education

Nuns in bodiless black and white
Pull your ear or slam a ruler
On your knuckles. You learn to be quiet
And behave. You learn to read,
You learn to dread.

Mornings in the classroom,
The nuns inspect what we write
On government-provided paper.
Their shadows fall upon us; we dare not
Look up. Beyond the classroom windows
The midday sun blazes
On the empty cement playground.

Inside the pueblo's cathedral,
Underneath the holy poses
Of elegant saints and Madonnas
Are cold flowers and incense, peasant prayers
Droning quiet centuries of tragedy.

The crucifix on the wall of the room
You share with your brother
Is the last thing you see before sleep.
You wake up to Christ's bloodied limbs
Welcoming you out of your dreams.

But this is another life I am speaking of, ours.

After lunch recess, I watch Mrs. Brady read
The book no one listens to.
Her voice makes prayers of Hardy Boys mysteries.

For Mrs. Brady it's a way to pass
Another hour of another afternoon
With the grandchildren of the Okies,
The Mexican kids who live in an alien
shared silence.

The crucifix still hangs on the bedroom wall.
At Saint Stanislaus the plaster saints
Of another country have always been at home
Under the agonized gaze of Christ crucified.
The afternoon light has no country.

GENEALOGY

The shifts at the canneries march workers in and out.

It is summer, when children drown in the irrigation canals.

The sun sleeps in the bodies of field workers,
their breathing makes a delicate music, like
the hum of traffic circling the suburbs.

At Crestwood Manor, Tracy Greer, who knows
she is Marilyn Monroe, walks the halls
in a fur coat, posing for invisible cameras.
Her beauty lives elsewhere.

The walls of Thomas Downey High School are blue.
At Crestwood Manor they are a washed out yellow.
The house of my childhood was painted pink
by my Mexican father. The pink has weathered
and the neighborhood has gone down.

At the Brave Bull bar, Lily, the skinny deaf drag queen,
sings Tammy Wynette's "Stand by your Man"
with a hand puppet of Kermit the Frog.

And Manuel Serrato, who once eclipsed
the beauty of every gay boy in town,
walks the streets with a dirty backpack.
Crack or madness embraces him. His disfiguring
screams mark an epic.

I have stopped by the 7-11 at 5:30 in the morning as
all the nights of the world were dying in its parking lot.
And knew that every night in the Valley
is a vigil leading to the same empty day.

I am a cartographer of the forgotten,
a chronicler of loss.

On the 99 Highway

Do not misunderstand, you are not the sole
owner of memory. Although you are the origin, the source
of those childhood afternoons in the Valley, hot summer days
without end, in your life, in the lives of many . . .

they, in the fields, under the scorching
weight of a phantom sun
continue the work you left them

generations will not distance the exhaustion
expended, in your name, in theirs

for nameless others

BORGES'S MIRROR

To face your immortality, Borges,

To enter the labyrinth of hexameters,
Virgil, swords, atlases, chess, encyclopedias,
The cities I have not known—Geneva and Austin, Texas,
Buenos Aires

To find a way back to
Baseball, disco music,
Modesto, the emptiness of the suburbs,
The *TV Guide*, Paperback novels, Hollywood movies,
Los Angeles and the Pacific,
Crucifixes, the Catholic colorfulness you loathed,
Baroque lyricisms rooted to your Whitman,
The great white shark of the television and movies

To evoke nostalgia
For the tigers of childhood
At the San Diego Zoo
And the night, the moon, the dreams
Infinitely doubled
Into blindness and recognition.

LADY WITH THE CATS

I don't want to see the lady a few houses down
Mistress of many cats, who drives a green Cadillac
No one knows anything about her
Keeper of an effortlessly guarded privacy

In what conspiracy of contentment
Does she live?
Her face is a soft meadow
Rippling in the late hours
Of the suburbs

LION'S BRIDGE

Crudely classic, resistant to gargoyleness,
Regal, zoo-savage, their roughly hewn

Fur grimed
By the coarse elements since 1916.

Their attentive sentinel stares
Like their insomniac brothers in Budapest, in European capitals,

These Modesto replicas.
Below their stiff stone manes

The Tuolumne River's staid waters slowly course
At the margins of the suburbs

Calling no poet's genius to dream songs of drowning
Or Okie Ophelia to its muddy currents

Mexican Narcissus faces an unloving backwater blankness.
Nonetheless, the lions' vacant eyes

Proudly fix on the landscape they lord over:
Trailer parks, billboards, roads without sidewalks, used car lots,

Canneries scenting the air with ketchupy humidity.
Year upon year, they withstand the poetry of negligence.

Blended to the wild unremarkable
Passed by, seen, but not noticed, welcoming

The crossing over to a
Kingdom of new mini-malls and parking lots.

JANIS JOPLIN AT HER HIGH SCHOOL REUNION

Sober and clean
    I mean to overcome

the small-town
    humiliations
of a fat girl
    with bad acne
    and a filthy mouth

now in my fame
in beads, bangles and boas
a scarred face

I hold my head up high
and put out of my mind
    the vomiting, the heaven of heroin
    Hippie San Francisco sinking in a swamp
        of Beat poetry and Southern Comfort

I see the prom queen,
    the wives,
  the forever cheerleaders
forever and ever amen
    the spirit of Texas, the Lone Star Republic

they are whispering,
smirking,
    condescending weird sisters

as if I was still
the misfit they knew

Oh, but alone I am not
the furies in blackface
are with me

mad guardians,
they'll lead me away from here

I won't be coming back

Larry Levis, Valley Poet

You were from the people
My people worked the fields for.

But the loneliness of the Valley,
Your essential aloneness,
Led to the Hades beyond the ranches
And the Mexicans—my fathers and uncles.

There, in the prodigal cities and towns of America,
In Oaxaca, Central Europe,
You reencountered the mute heart of the Valley—
The manic emptiness, frenzied isolation,
The daemons of lyricism, the furies of genius.

The stars and the skies of the San Joaquin followed you
In the ungrounded night.
And always, in the glory of distance,
The shadow glamour of rupture,
Death, your coming home.

III. THE CHRONICLES

CHRONICLES

i. immigration

Dad is again in *el norte.*
Letters and telegrams bring him back to us.
In her garden Mother pours over his words.
The waiting over, documents secured,
he's taking us with him next time.

The roses are blooming,
butterflies are in season,
a rabid dog is loose in the streets.
Scorpions and garden snakes
lurk in the shadows.

Church bells travel
the afternoon silence.

Mother prays.

ii. Vietnam

There is no other world yet.
We walk, my brother and I,
to where the pueblo
becomes plains of trees and cacti.
We shoot at hummingbirds
with rocks flung from slingshots.
They are beautiful,
these hummingbirds,
but still we want to kill them.
In town arrive long-haired American
men people call Alleluyas.
They come because they refuse
to go to war. They are escaping
a country we'll soon be going to.

iii. glam rock

My parents' work clothes
smell of the sun and the fields,
the juices of ripe peaches
picked in the afternoon heat.
It is summer. The family
watches *The Ten Commandments*
on the television: God's drama,
utterly absorbing.
On the news after the movie
homosexuals are marching
in San Francisco, carrying signs
in opposition to a California
proposition. Later, in the dark, alone,
I watch David Bowie on
Saturday Night Live.
Ziggy Stardust is not man or woman,
he's dazzling, otherworldly, glittery.
He scares me, he's fascinating.

iv. icons

Jerry Falwell is pointing
at a map of Central America,
a smug grin on his face.
Stick in hand, he traces
communism's covert crawl from
Cuba to El Salvador, through Guatemala,
to Mexico, into California,
to take over the United States.
Communism is the great evil,
President Reagan's enthusiasm
for the Contras, the freedom fighters,
is approved of by God.
On the Spanish language channel
I have watched peasant women in El Salvador
pouring lamentations into the graves
of loved ones.
At church on Sunday prayers are dedicated
to nuns raped in the war zones;
another group of priests
have been murdered in El Salvador.
It is the first years of MTV.
Madonna is wearing rosaries,
an excess of accessories.
She still has body fat.
She has not yet grabbed her
crotch. I know this Catholic

ghetto girl from Michigan is
an icon, an image
of beauty and promise.

MEXICO

Indelible afternoons of a childhood
In the country of his blood and of his
Forefathers. It will never be foreign,
What became memory

Without explanation or reason.
They came to an end: the scent
Of the lemon trees, the days ordered
By the angelus, the scorpions,

The pueblo's family histories . . .
He long ago gave up lamenting.
There are misfortunes more important
And more difficult to overcome.

The sun does not obey time.
He remembers: Mexico's afternoons,
Innocent and dead, the boy he was
The man he would have been.

MENTAL HEALTH WORKER AT CRESTWOOD MANOR

Underneath the layers of make-up
is the face of a beautiful Indian woman,
ancient and strong,
mythically Mayan.

She takes care of the old crazy people
eight hours a night
washing, cleaning them
as if they were her children.
Days of babysitting insanity have
convalesced any *locura*
survived in her blood.

She helps the old ones
put on nightgowns,
tucks them into bed,
watches their insanity
rest in their sleep
as she counts the dreamless hours,
checks on them once in a while
to make sure they are not dead or awake.
It does not matter
if it is a full moon
or a half-moon outside.
It's a living,
this ritual vigil.

When the dawn arrives,
her patients revived
to their torments of wakefulness,
she punches her timecard,
drives home to dress
her children for school,
and to prepare her husband's lunch
while the moon refuses to leave
the early morning.

At home, the silence of her kitchen
is a continuation of the stillness
in the mental ward—
but the moon outside is now absent.

She goes to bed alone.

HOMOSEXUAL REPRESSION

The first time was a boy in an elevator
He looked at me first
As the elevator went up

It couldn't be stopped
After that

Came boys in bathrooms and motel rooms
Never in my hometown
Where I'm known

Where it's hard to resist
Because they're everywhere
Always they are teenagers
At a mall, the supermarket, the 7-11
All it takes is a glance
They know you by instinct
Know what you're capable of
How far you will go

The black boys hate you and want you
And expect to be paid
The Mexicans pretend to be sweet
Too proud to ask for money
But they'll rip you off in the end
The worst are the cynical white kids
Pale flat chests the same as my sons'
As I become father and predator to them

There was one I couldn't get enough of
In Tucson, a Mexican with liquid eyes
And skin soft as a girl's

Oh, he was just like a girl, his brown beauty
Mocked my wife's rich fading prettiness

We'd meet in motel rooms with
Pictures of impressionist water lilies on the walls
Sunsets or beachscapes
In which nature is pretty and kind
And nothing ever goes wrong

I loved him, Miguel,
He could hardly speak English
He had nothing
I wanted to give him
The hate of my kids, the shame of my wife
The disgust of my buddies
The gossipy whispers of all the people I know

I was willing to destroy all that I was for him
But all he wanted was to be touched
Made love to
By a stranger

Los Angeles, 3:24 p.m.

There are days when the downtown air
is heavy with the smog of psychosis,
a thousand schizophrenic souls walking the streets.
Something of their madness is carried in the cacophony
of salsa music and bad pop *en español* from cheap shops on Broadway,
in the shrieking of the Guatemalan preacher woman
warning of damnation and repentance and competing with police sirens,
the strident humming of traffic.

The air is thick with the day's weight of despair
junkies dream junkie dreams
their alchemizing of the afternoon light,
while immigrants pray, enraptured by holy fantasies
inside the State Theatre, old baroque movie house,
now the Pare de Sufrir church on 7th and Broadway.

Afternoons when flesh longs for flesh
in the madness of the maddening air,
and some dream because they can't help it,
others because they're addicted,
and there are the Mexican and Central American parents
on Broadway buying back-to-school clothes for their kids,
the black girl crying on the pay phone,
the overcrowded buses,
the elderly Koreans in the Van Nuys building on Spring Street
waiting for death to take them somewhere else,
the Maoists at Libros Revolución dreaming of bloody revolts—
you can feel the lunatic tension

its incalculable elemental submersion in the downtown streets,
and there are those in love,
and those longing to die,
and those chosen for simple happiness,
and the young Latina girls staking their lives on their prettiness,
and the cholos at home in the downtown streets
as much as in jail.

And at the Alexander Hotel on 5th and Spring
Pepe Rodriguez, old matador,
star of Mexican bullrings of the 50s and 60s
was found strangled:
the walls of his rent-by-the-day room
plastered with photographs of Pepe
during his famed bullfighting days.

THE SOUTHERN PACIFIC RAILROAD TRAIN

Train tracks
traverse the patternless suburbs.

The train's wheels churn
into the flat soundlessness
of the San Joaquin Valley.

Factories emptied of industry
and desiccated peach fields.
In other states of the Republic falling snow
brightens the night of a freezing season.
Here, fog moves in the snowless dark
going nowhere. It stays close to
the earth, as if pulled to it.

The fog makes driving dangerous:
it consumes headlights, obscures parking lots.

The sound of the train's whistle recedes
into the silence
the distances of fog.

Working people are home.
Inside the heated tract houses
the air is greasy with fried food.
Televisions are on: laugh tracks, remote wars,
music videos, police in Los Angeles staging arrests.

The train has gone deep into the fog.
The whistle of the next train will sound in five hours,
like a slight lament, and won't be heard
except by insomniacs.
The train's movement is another kind of sleep.

LOS ANGELES, 1992

The parrots were set free
by the riot's chaos
bright plumage
plunging into smoke and ash
as they flew above
        smoldering buildings

Their old captivity
transformed by flames
as pet shops burned
animals entered the wild
        bewildered by liberty

BOHEMIA

I live in a converted bank downtown
In the third world of Los Angeles:

A small studio, a fourth floor view
Of the backside of an abandoned building
Where sunlight gathers and diffuses
On the century-old brick wall
On windows darkened with grime
Or covered up with boards

Junkies shoot up in the piss-stinking alley
That movie crews hose down
For filming, now and then
To transform it into New York,
A futuristic cyborg city, or backdrop
To some music video

And I ask myself
What has brought me here?
To the forgotten and faked
To what the cities have chewed up
Or hallucinate?

I long for trees and children
For what my vagrant soul spurned

I long for suburbs
Other unlivable landscapes.

Intimacy

It is always a foreign city
At 2:30 in the morning
In rooms that remind us
We are strangers.

Sometimes more than one language
Is awkwardly at work
One doesn't entirely understand the other
And it doesn't matter

It will be over before too much is said
And what was not understood is soon forgotten.
Still, shame, fear, enters

And passes, like a quick intake of breath,
One or the other will pull out a condom and there will be
More talk or not much talking, and some uneasiness.

The room is a few stories up, and because
Your mind is preoccupied, you're not sure
How many. What the hallway looked like will be
Forgotten, and the stairs or the elevator, but not

How one got there, in his car, a taxi, or walking
Unfamiliar streets. One knows more about him

From what's in the room than from what he says.
Sometimes there are family photos near a desk, strangers
Smiling in a time and place he forever shares

With them, and he will point out his father
Or a sister, or else pretend the photos aren't there, as if
They looked accusingly upon the scene.

When there are no family photos the room seems colder
And yet more accommodating to the conspiracy, the tenderness.
Afterward, you will remember or not remember

How he kissed. It was summer, or winter . . . the time of year
Will remain clear, but not the color of his eyes.
From the window you see buildings, empty sidewalks,

Cars in the streets—the loneliness
You came from and will find your way back to.
It will be years before

You think of that night again:
You are driving on the 101 and remember
The dark blue sweater he removed in the half-dark,

And in the morning, what was it that he said?
Thank you, Goodbye, Nice to have met you:
Every gesture, every word collapses, meaningless

Faithful to the night that has ended.
I won't do this again
Or not for a while. I must go . . . there's no need

To be ashamed, oh, the light is bright outside,
We did nothing wrong, it was good, it was safe.
Goodbye, why is smiling so difficult?
He had a nice face.

HIGH WINDS

From the airplane's window, a view of the fires
edging the ranges near the ocean,
brownish-gray smoke displaces clouds.
The plane descends through the dark smog of
the blazes, tiny in the distance, like flames from matches.

The Santa Ana winds buttress the burning
at the edges of the Southland.
The evacuated gather at football stadiums.

Mad circulation of traffic, as usual.
The war. Upcoming elections. Britney Spears.
A light comedy, a commercial, are being filmed downtown.
The rich yellow texture of the light,
like stained glass. The fires.

Woman from John Berryman's "Dream Song 4"

"—Black hair, complexion Latin, jeweled eyes . . ."

They claim a right to look at you,
       to have you in their thoughts.
       He's tense and disheveled.
I recognize him from pictures in the papers.
       He looks like a man

who doesn't know how to swim in his lust.
       I wish he'd turn away.
       The darkness in the restaurant
       seems to search him out.
    I know that kind of man; he gives himself
         to the shadows
      of all he cannot reach.
           I am the flesh of the darkness
           he hungers.

LOOKING FOR GOD IN LOS ANGELES

I have figured it out.
Everyone in Los Angeles is looking for God.
Nobody knows it, but everyone is trying to touch God.
The divorced man who works out twice a day at the YMCA

is certainly looking for God.
And the young blond girls with identical plastic surgery noses
at The Standard Hotel downtown are looking for God.
The gangsters murdering themselves are just trying to find God.

In LA, even the young and the beautiful are lonely,
and their loneliness is a reaching out to God.
Yes, beauty is frightening in the city of angels,
absolute, promising everything,

but completely unaccountable,
because beauty belongs to God,
and God is somewhere else,
outside the beautiful.

Death is the only thing that has found God in LA,
but nobody believes it,
nobody believes in death.

The Seasons

November heat. Confusion of seasons:
Summer lingers, summer's emptiness.

Who were once lovers
Grow older in distant cities
Addresses have long been lost
Their lives are hearsay
Their faces like traces of photographs
In unread newspapers in coffee shops.

He remembers his fine Gallic face
Ravaged by youth, by a time that
Would not last. Curiosity or nostalgia
Bring back that summer:
A student dorm room in Santa Cruz
A boat on Pier 39
Yosemite National Park—
The first taste of the void
Otherwise known as the first time
The unrepeatable death.

It is the middle of life,
When friends have started to die.

November heat. Arrested autumn.
The change of season that doesn't arrive.

FIRST RAINS AFTER SUMMER

Warm rain, intruder upon the last
Sighs of summer. The waters given to waste
Exhale the months of heat and shared desire:

The sun and bright mornings wakened to lovers.
They are no more. It is autumn and the spent
Leaves fall elsewhere. We are one year
Older, and not wiser or more sane.

The city sidewalks—humid, faithless, soiled—
Are drenched in a tropical slick slumber. I walk,
After the tentative music of raindrops has settled,
Alone, remembering the days

Still fresh, when rain was unimaginable
And our bodies slept next to each other.

Henry James and My Mother

Mother would not give in
to fear, the nameless menaces.

I wonder who knew more happiness.
The master, who banqueted on tragedy and beauty,
or my mother, who anchored her sanity
to sacrifice, the bringing up of children.

They were both exiles of sorts.
A boundless solitude, ruthless
and uncommon,
pursued them.

Neither knew flesh
for the sake of the flesh,
the sacred waste of salvation,
the giving surrender
to that terrible wonder, the lover.

I think their grace was equal,
let the books say what they will.
Devoid of nostalgia for the country she left,
like Henry James, she accepted the
foreign country of her fate.
In Modesto, her Mexican calla lilies
abundantly took root in suburban soil.

While he, among the metropolitan
whispers and innuendos of another century,
stalked the gilded mirrors of his loneliness.

And now it is the age of isolation.
I am my mother's son,
I never noticed her flowers.

The master, whose untoward splendor
disinherits me, is an uneasy father,
I live him in all my incapable loves.

THE PRODIGAL SON'S FAMILY

They never thought to ask themselves
What would lead him away from
All he had known—all that was
Supposed to be enough—

To live alone, amidst the glitter and
Deprivation of cities, on roads avoided
And unknown, and houses never meant
To be a home. They never thought

To ask themselves why he would
Return, his face transformed
By pleasure and distance.
They never thought to question

The despair in his eyes, the difficult
Smile in the family photographs
And why his presence among
Them is so alien, and permanent.

BIOGRAPHICAL NOTE

The author of *Other Countries* (What Books Press, 2010) and *Ricardo Valverde* (University of Minnesota Press, 2013), Ramón García has published poetry in a variety of journals and anthologies including *Best American Poetry 1996*, *Ambit*, *The Floating Borderlands: Twenty-Five Years of US-Hispanic Literature* (1998), *Crab Orchard Review*, *Poetry Salzburg Review*, *Los Angeles Review*, and *Mandorla: New Writing from the Americas*. A founding member of the Glass Table Collective, an artist collective formed in 2008, he is a professor at California State University, Northridge, and lives in Los Angeles.

www.ingramcontent.com/pod-product-compliance
Lightning Source LLC
Chambersburg PA
CBHW022012080426
42733CB00007B/572